W9-BRN-780

Contents

Acknowledgments

This book is dedicated to my family, Richie, Paige, and Matthew. Thank you for your patience through the long nights and weekends of sewing, sketching, and writing. I love you very much and could not have written this book without your continued support and inspiration.

Thank you to my parents, Jim and Karen Smisek, for believing in everything I do. Mom, thank you for teaching me how to sew at such a young age. Love you lots!

Thank you to Susanne Woods, Liz Aneloski, and everyone else at C&T Publishing / Stash Books who was able to see my vision and support me through the publishing process. You all rock!

Thank you to all my family, friends, and co-workers for all the encouragement and assurance you provided when it was needed most.

Thank you to Moda Fabrics and Ty Pennington Fabrics for graciously providing fabrics used in this book.

Fabrics from the following companies were also used in the projects:

Alexander Henry Fabrics

Clothworks

FreeSpirit Fabrics

Henry Glass Fabrics

Michael Miller Fabrics

Riley Blake Designs

Robert Kaufman Fabrics

Timeless Treasures Fabrics

The following are notion manufacturers featured in this book; their products can be found at your local fabric and quilt stores:

A&E (American & Efird)

Dritz

Fairfield Processing

Mary Ellen Products

Pellon

Sewline Products

I use Janome Memory Craft 6500P and Janome Serger 1100D sewing machines.

Introduction

Having two children, a girl and a boy, I quickly found how easy it was to find many projects for girls but hardly any for boys. This became quite frustrating yet very inspiring at the same time. Sure, you can find the traditional baby boy patterns that feature a blue train, puppy dog, and rattle. But what about the toddlers, teens, and even the "big boys"?

I am often inspired by the everyday items we encounter throughout our lives. When I was working up the concept for this book, I wanted the projects in it to be something that boys of all ages would enjoy receiving or even learning to make for themselves. All the guys in my life have always been big into cars. Even my son, from the time he could pick up things with his little hands, first reached for a little toy car. So, with that in mind, I began to brainstorm on the little elements that coincide with cars and

transportation. Then it hit me—traffic signs and signals! Nothing could be more fitting.

I enjoy working with various types of fabrics and creating a texture and depth with simple cottons. When I first came up with the idea of creating a scrap appliqué, I was trying to find a way to incorporate many of the fabric prints that I loved into a single application. Rather than just using a solid flat piece of fabric, why not create a "fabric" from the often-neglected scraps of material that get set aside in hopes of using them in a future project? This idea then transformed into sewing together 2½″ strips, such as strips from a Bella Solid Jelly Roll, to give a quilt or other project more texture.

In this book, you will learn how to create a new style of scrap appliqué and apply this technique to twelve fun and exciting projects designed especially with the boys in mind.

Angela Yosten

Some Basic Information

The Tools and Supplies

I will refer to some of the tools listed below throughout the book. Whether you are a newbie to appliqué or an experienced professional, you can check back here as often as you like to get a better understanding of what you are working with.

Closures: Buttons, grommets, hooks, snaps, and zippers are are used in this book. It is always fun to experiment with new ways for using traditional closures. I usually use Dritz products.

Fabrics: Using quality fabrics is key to having a long-lasting quilt or project that you can cherish for many years.

Fillers: Pillow forms, quilt batting, and stuffing are the most commonly used fillers in the industry. Typically, these items are made of a cotton/polyester blend; however, new technologies have made natural fibers such as soy, bamboo, and natural cotton widely used. Pillow forms make stuffing a pillow fast and easy without all the mess of loose fiberfill stuffing. Quilt batting is a thin, soft layer that is placed between a quilt top and backing to create warmth and comfort. I use Luna batting (Moda) and Fairfield pillow forms.

Fusible Web: A staple in appliqué, this paper-backed, double-sided adhesive makes sewing appliqué, both large and small shapes, a breeze. Activated by the heat of an iron, the adhesive helps keep the appliqué fused to the project while you stitch around the raw edges. I use Wonder-Under (Pellon).

Interfacing: Fusible interfacings help add necessary weight and stability to fabrics where needed. They come in various weights and thicknesses to work in any project. I use fast2fuse and Shape-Flex (C&T Publishing).

Needles: You need a sewing needle to hand stitch openings closed on some of the projects. Any size hand needle will do.

Point Turner: Having a good point turner can really make a difference when turning sharp corners on a project. Point turners are made specifically to help push out a corner on a bag, pillow, and more when flipping the fabric right side out. Don't use your scissors to push out the corners as this could damage your project. I use the Classic Crystal Point Turner (Lee) and Alex Anderson's 4-in-1 Essential Sewing Tool (C&T Publishing).

Rotary Cutter: Rotary cutters come in a few sizes; one of the most commonly used is a 45mm rotary cutter. Be sure to always have a sharp blade to help maintain perfect cutting every time. I use Omnigrid rotary cutters.

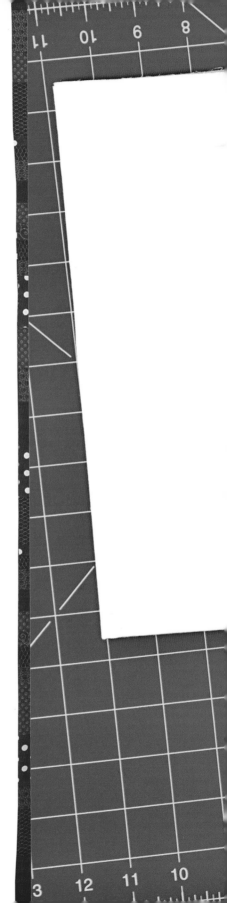

Rotary Cutting Mat: A self-healing rotary mat with grid-lines is used in conjunction with the rotary cutter and ruler. These tools will help make your cutting go much quicker. I use Omnigrid mats.

Rotary Ruler: I personally like to use an 8½″ × 24″ ruler; however, any width × 24″ will work great. I use Omnigrid rulers.

Scissors: Two sharp pairs of fabric scissors (both long and short) are essential to cutting out all the curves and corners on your appliqué. Never use your fabric scissors on paper.

Seam Ripper: Everyone makes mistakes once in a while, so be sure to have a seam ripper on hand for those unwanted oopsies.

Spray Starch: Using a good spray starch will help you press out those wrinkles and folds in your fabrics. I use Best Press (Mary Ellen Products).

Straight Pins: Straight pins are very useful in holding fabrics together while sewing at your machine. Pull those pins out before you get to them, and don't sew over your pins as you may break your machine needle.

Tape Measure: An extra-long flexible tape measure will come in handy for the larger projects in this book.

Templates: Patterns for the projects are supplied either at the end of a project or on the pullout pages included with this book. Hint: Trace the patterns on tracing paper or the paper-backed fusible web to maintain the original patterns for multiple uses. I use Sewline marking tools.

Thread: Several kinds of threads are available in the quilting and sewing industry. A good-quality thread, such as Mettler Metrosene (from A&E), will last a lifetime and will not split or break while sewing.

The Scrap Bucket

Whether we use a bag, basket, or bucket, we all have some place we're storing pieces of fabric. Our containers hold lots and lots of leftover scraps that are waiting patiently for their day to be used in a quilt, bag, or embellishment. I personally have a difficult time discarding my little joys of fabric. Why should their larger counterparts have all the fun and be showcased in a sewing project while the small scraps just get shoved aside? Well, their day has finally come, and they will soon be stitched into your next project.

The first thing to do is to dump all those lovely scraps onto the floor and start sorting them by color. This process will make it much more convenient when searching for scraps in a certain colorway. Place each pile of colored scraps in a separate zipper storage bag. These see-through bags make finding the right colors quick and easy when working on your projects. Store all your color-separated bags back in your favorite scrap bag, basket, or bucket.

TIP Having a place for everything and organizing your fabrics by color helps make your sewing experience that much more enjoyable.

CREATING SCRAP APPLIQUÉ

What is a scrap appliqué? Many would define it as a small piece of scrap fabric cut into a shape and either hand or machine sewn to another piece of fabric or article of clothing. While this method is very useful and can achieve several interesting looks, I prefer to take a more modern approach to this term by stitching several pieces of fabric together to create a new style of appliqué. Every project in this book uses the following technique to create each scrap appliqué.

1. Create scraps by cutting various sized strips from yardage or your scrap stash.

2. Sew similarly colored scraps together in strips to create a fabric base for the appliqué. (This can also be called strip piecing.)

3. Press the seam allowances in the same direction; topstitching the seams is optional.

4. Trace the template pattern onto the paper side of the fusible web.

5. Trim around the traced pattern, leaving a little extra around the outside of the edge. Fuse the trimmed fusible web to the wrong side of the strip-pieced fabric base. Cut out the appliqué shapes, and remove the paper backing.

TIP All appliqué templates provided for the projects in this book have already been reversed for fusible scrap appliqué. Simply, trace, cut, fuse, and stitch.

6. Apply the scrap appliqués to the background fabric or on other scrap appliqué base shapes as directed in each project by fusing them in place with a hot iron. Using your favorite style of decorative stitching, stitch around each piece to complete the appliqué.

Throughout the book I use two appliqué techniques, machine appliqué and reverse appliqué. Machine appliqué is a quick and durable method for sewing the appliqué shapes directly to the foundation fabric. The foundation fabric remains hidden behind the appliqué shape. **Reverse appliqué** is created when you place the appliqué on top of the foundation fabric and cut away part of the top layer of fabric to reveal the foundation fabric under it. Both methods add lots of depth and texture and are beneficial in their own ways. There is no need to turn under the appliqué raw edges because you will hide the edges with zigzag, satin, or buttonhole stitches. For a raw-edge look, simply sew a straight stitch close to the edge of the fabric to hold the appliqué in place.

TIP

Don't be afraid to mix and match different sizes, weights, and textures of fabrics. Doing this can really make your project stand out and be unique.

Binding

Binding a quilt is an essential last step to finish the edges. It is what completes the quilt and gives a clean, finished look so that it can be cherished for years to come.

1. Cut 2½˝-wide binding strips as directed in the instructions for the quilt.

2. Lay 2 strips end to end at 90° with right sides together. Draw a diagonal line from corner to corner and stitch on that line. Trim to a ¼˝ seam allowance and press the seam allowances open. Continue until all the strips are sewn together. (Figure A)

3. Cut the beginning end of the long binding strip at a 45° angle, fold the trimmed end to the wrong side, and press. Trim the overhanging tail. (Figure B)

4. Fold the long strip in half lengthwise with wrong sides together and press. (Figure C)

5. On the right side of the quilt, starting on the top edge, match up the raw edges of the binding to the raw edges of the quilt. Backstitch and stitch with a ⅜˝ seam allowance starting about 4˝–6˝ in from the beginning (trimmed) end of the binding.

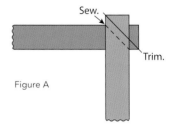

Sew.

Trim.

Figure A

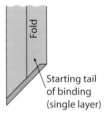

Fold

Starting tail of binding (single layer)

Figure B

Figure C

6. Stitch along the top of the quilt. When you reach ⅜″ from the corner of the quilt, backstitch, and then remove the quilt from the machine. (Figure D)

7. Fold the tail of the binding up so that it forms a 45° angle, then back down, aligning the binding raw edges with the raw edge of the quilt. (Figures E and F) Press.

8. Begin stitching again from the corner.

9. Continue to stitch and fold at each corner until you come back almost to where you started. Stop about 4″ before you reach the starting point and backstitch. Remove the quilt from the machine.

10. Overlap the beginning and ending binding tails and trim the ending tail at a 90° angle, keeping a small overlap where the ending tail is covered by the beginning tail.

11. Insert the ending tail of the binding strip into the "pocket" of the folded beginning tail. (Figure G)

12. Stitch down the remaining section of binding, sewing slightly beyond the starting stitches.

13. Fold the binding to the quilt back and hand stitch, mitering the corners.

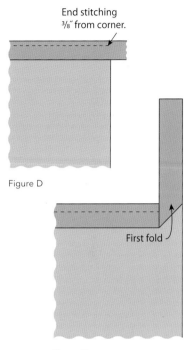

End stitching ⅜″ from corner.

First fold

Figure D

Figure E

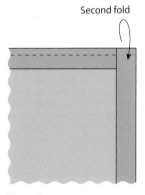

Second fold

Figure F

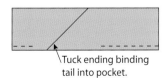

Tuck ending binding tail into pocket.

Figure G

Inspired by the simple pages found in a coloring book, the solid-colored strip-pieced base allows this traditional traffic light to be the main attraction.

green light GO
red light STOP

Traffic Light
WALLHANGING QUILT

Finished quilt: APPROXIMATELY 42″ × 62″

Materials

1 solid Jelly Roll (Moda #9900JR 11) or 32 off-white strips 2½″ × width of fabric for the background fabric

2½″ strips of assorted fabric scraps* in black, red, green, and yellow for the scrap appliqués:

Black: 8 strips at least 29″ long

Red: 4 strips at least 10″ long

Green: 4 strips at least 10″ long

Yellow: 4 strips at least 10″ long and 2 strips at least 26″ long

2 yards of coordinating fabric for backing

½ yard of coordinating fabric for binding

1¾ yards of fusible web

46″ × 66″ of quilt batting

*Note: I used narrower strips in my quilt. This is okay as long as you make the scrap appliqué base the correct overall size. You can also join short strips together along their short ends to create longer strips.

Background

All seams are ¼″ unless otherwise noted.

1. Sew the 32 off-white strips together along their long edges using a ¼″ seam allowance, creating a background.

STRAIGHT STRIPS

When sewing your 2½″ strips together, make sure the ends match up so you don't get a curve in your finished piece. Match the very tops together, stitch about ½″, and then stop. Make sure your needle is in the down position, and then pull the strips so that the center folds match on each strip. Hold the strips together while sewing to these folds. With your needle in the down position, pull the strips again so that the bottoms of the strips match up. Hold in place while you finish sewing to the bottom of the strips. Alternate the ends where you start stitching and repeat for each strip.

2. Press all the seam allowances in the same direction. Don't topstitch along the seamlines at this point.

Scrap Appliqué

See Creating Scrap Appliqué (page 13) for detailed instructions. Traffic Light patterns are on pages 23–27 and are reversed for fusible scrap appliqué.

1. Group the 2½˝ strips by color. Sew each color group of strips together to achieve approximately the following sizes:

Black: 16½˝ × 29˝

Red: 8½˝ × 10˝

Green: 8½˝ × 10˝

Yellow: 8½˝ × 10˝ and 4½˝ × 25˝

2. Press all the seam allowances in the same direction on each color set.

   Optional: Topstitch the seams down.

3. Create half of the black A1 pattern on tracing paper: Trace patterns A1a and A1b, placing them 18″ apart with their centerlines in alignment. Draw the joining centerline 18″ long. Draw the outside edge extension line to connect the 2 patterns. This creates half of the traffic light. Trace the outside edges of the half pattern onto the paper side of the fusible web; then flip the tracing paper pattern and continue tracing the other half onto the fusible web.

4. Trace the remaining Traffic Light patterns onto the paper side of the fusible web. You will make multiple copies of some of the patterns.

5. Loosely cut around each of the fusible web templates. Position and iron the traced templates to the backside of the appropriate colored fabrics:

   Black: A1, g-r-e-e-n, l-i-g-h-t, r-e-d, and l-i-g-h-t

   Red: A2 and S-T-O-P

   Green: A2 and G-O

   Yellow: A2 and A3

6. Carefully cut out the fabric appliqués on the traced lines, and remove the paper backing. Trim the bottom part of the yellow light stand to approximately 4″ × 25″. Fuse the appliqués in place on the background and on other appliqué base pieces. (Remember to fuse both pieces of the yellow light stand in place.)

Note

Slightly overlap the edges of adjacent appliqué shapes to avoid gaps.

Finishing

1. Sandwich the backing fabric, batting, and quilt top, and safety pin baste the layers together.

Note

The width of your backing fabric may be slightly narrower than the quilt top. This is okay. Just try to match them up as closely as possible. You will trim down all the sides to match after the quilting is done.

2. Machine appliqué around the pieces with your favorite stitch. I chose a small buttonhole stitch.

3. To complete the quilting, topstitch along the background seams, skipping over the appliquéd pieces.

4. Using a rotary cutter, mat, and ruler, square up the corners and trim off any excess fabric from all 4 sides of the quilt. Be sure both sides are parallel.

5. From the binding fabric, cut 6 strips 2½˝ × width of fabric. Trim off all the selvages.

6. Refer to Binding (page 16) to create and add the binding.

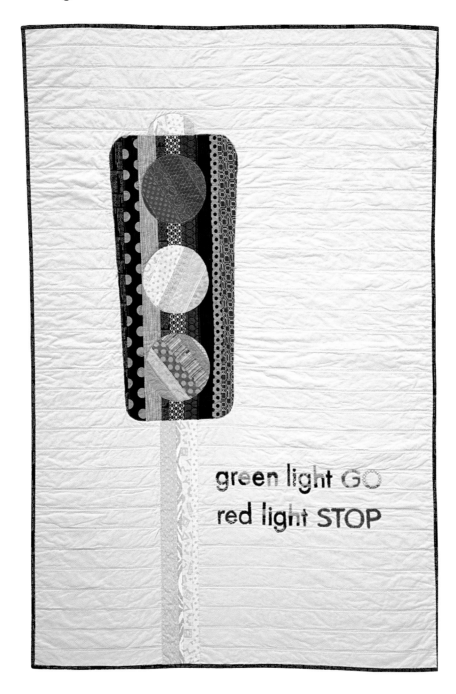

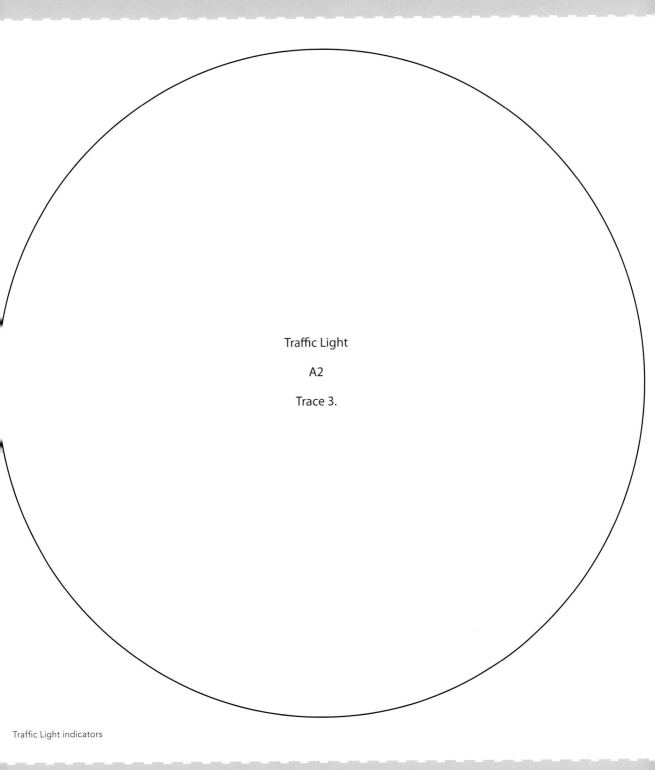

Traffic Light

A2

Trace 3.

Traffic Light indicators

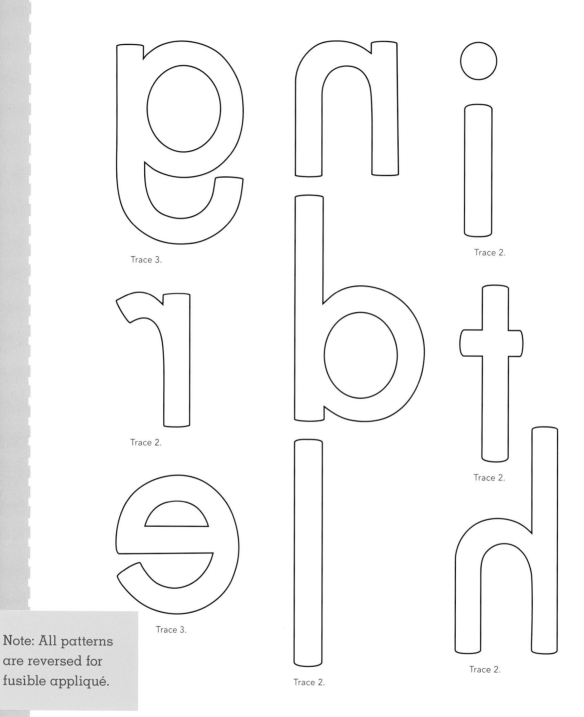

Trace 3.

Trace 2.

Trace 2.

Trace 2.

Trace 3.

Trace 2.

Trace 2.

Note: All patterns are reversed for fusible appliqué.

Traffic Light text

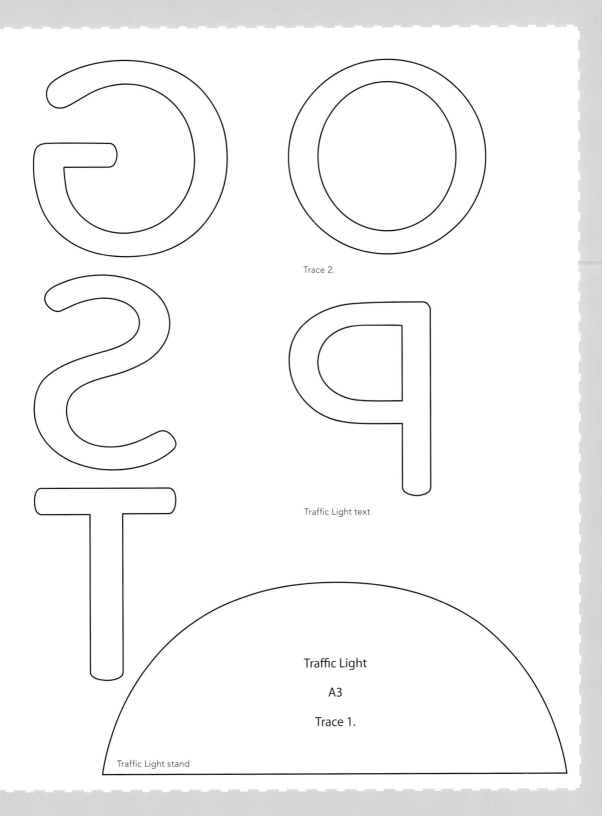

Trace 2.

Traffic Light text

Traffic Light

A3

Trace 1.

Traffic Light stand

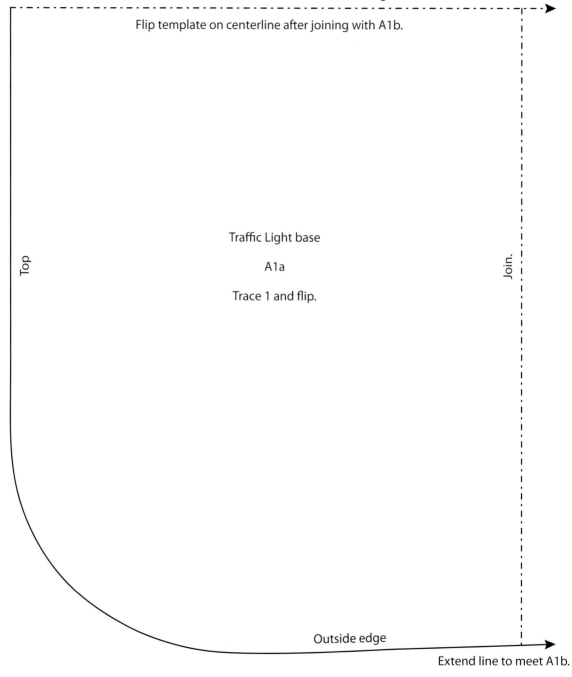

Align with A1b, and extend line 18″.

Flip template on centerline after joining with A1b.

Traffic Light base

A1a

Trace 1 and flip.

Top

Join.

Outside edge

Extend line to meet A1b.

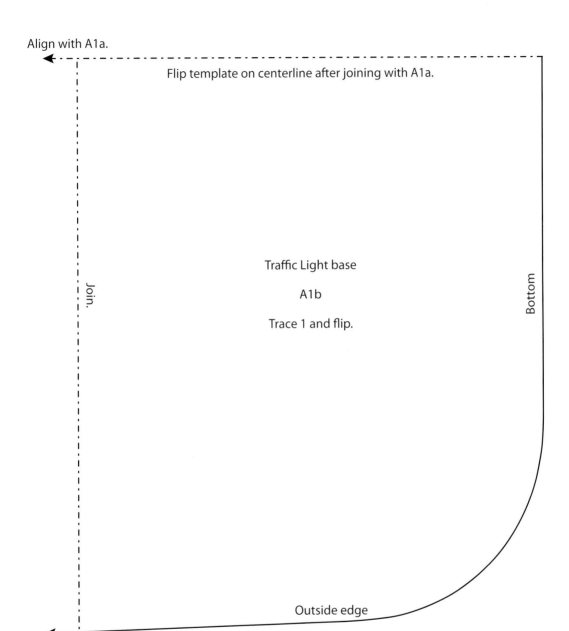

Align with A1a.

Flip template on centerline after joining with A1a.

Join.

Traffic Light base

A1b

Trace 1 and flip.

Bottom

Outside edge

Extend to meet A1a.

Traffic Light base

To create half of the Traffic Light base pattern on tracing paper, trace the bottom corner, draw a straight line 18˝ along the centerline, and add the top corner, aligning the centerlines. Draw a line to join the outside edges. Trace this half-pattern on fusible web, flip the pattern, and trace the second half on the fusible web. Note the bottom traffic light base (A1b) is narrower than the top piece (A1a).

A "reversible" pillowcase
can make a great addition
to every boy's bed. Stop one
day and Go the next ... all
in one pillow.

Stop and Go
PILLOWCASE

Finished pillowcase: APPROXIMATELY 21″ × 32″

Materials

⅞ yard for pillowcase body; trim to 27″ × WOF (width of fabric)

½ yard for flange; trim to 13″ × WOF

⅛ yard for accent trim; trim to 2½″ × WOF

Strips of assorted fabric scraps in red and green for the letter scrap appliqués

⅛ yard of fusible web

Standard pillow

Pillowcase

All seams are ½″ unless otherwise noted.

1. Fold and press the flange fabric in half lengthwise, wrong sides together (6½″ × WOF).

2. Topstitch ¼″ from the fold. Set aside.

3. Fold and press the accent trim fabric in half lengthwise, wrong sides together (1¼″ × WOF). Set aside.

4. Place the pillowcase body fabric right side up with the 27″ dimension along the side. Place the long raw edges of the accent trim fabric along the top long raw edge of the pillowcase body fabric. Place the long raw edges of the flange fabric on top of the pillowcase body fabric, sandwiching the accent trim between the pillowcase body and flange fabrics.

5. Pin and stitch with a ½″ seam allowance. Zigzag or serge the raw edge for a clean finish.

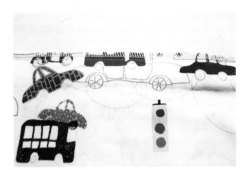

6. From the right side, open the stitched fabrics and press the accent trim piece toward the pillowcase body. Topstitch ⅛″ from the seam on the flange side, catching the seam allowances.

Scrap Appliqué

See Creating Scrap Appliqué (page 13) for detailed instructions. Stop and Go (pillowcase) patterns are on page 32 and are reversed for fusible scrap appliqué.

1. Group the colored strips by color. Sew each color group of strips together to achieve approximately the following sizes:

Red: approximately 5″ × 5″

Green: approximately 5″ × 5″

2. Press all the seam allowances in the same direction.

   Optional: Topstitch the seams down.

3. Trace the letter- patterns onto the paper side of the fusible web.

4. Loosely cut around the fusible web templates. Position and iron the traced templates to the backside of the appropriate scrap-pieced fabrics:

Green: g-o.

Red: s-t-o-p.

5. Carefully cut out the fused templates on the traced lines, and remove the paper backing.

6. Fold the pillowcase in half, with wrong sides together and matching selvages, and fuse an appliqué word on each side of the pillowcase. I placed "stop." about 4″ from the bottom and 3″ from

Finishing

the selvages and "go." about 4″ from the bottom and 2″ from the fold. Before fusing, check the alignment of the letters, making sure the words are upright and readable when the pillowcase is turned over or "reversed."

1. Fold the pillowcase wrong sides together, matching the selvages. Stitch ¼″ inside the bottom raw edges and side selvage edges, pivoting at the corner with the needle down.

2. Carefully clip the 2 bottom corners to reduce bulk.

3. Turn the pillowcase wrong side out. Press.

4. Stitch ⅜″ in from the bottom and side edges, pivoting at the stitched side seam. Do not clip the corners. Turn the pillowcase right side out and insert the pillow.

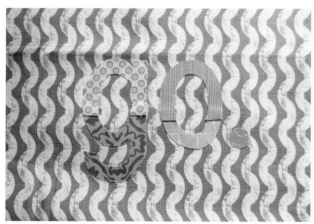

7. Unfold the pillowcase to one layer. Machine appliqué around the pieces with your favorite stitch. I chose a small buttonhole stitch.

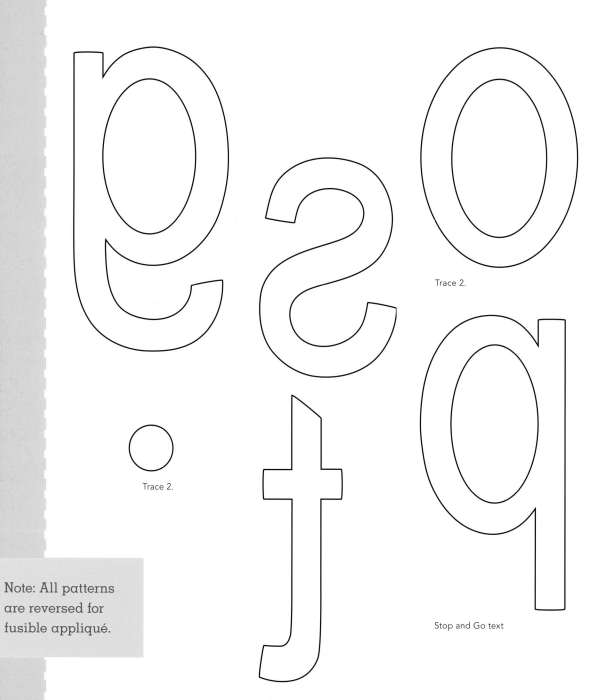

Trace 2.

Trace 2.

Stop and Go text

Note: All patterns are reversed for fusible appliqué.

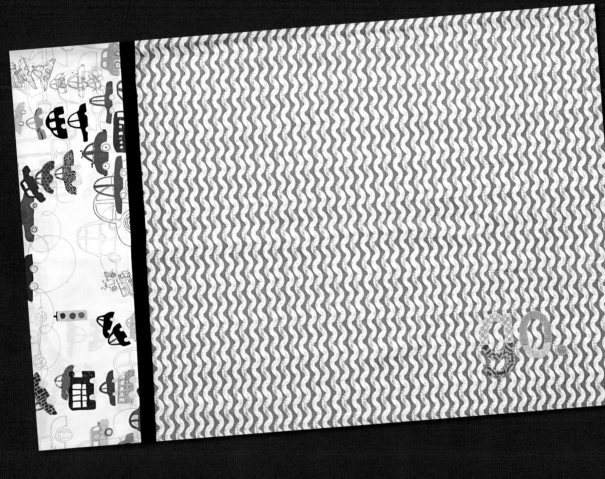

Make a bold statement with a No Parking sign on a duvet cover made from twin-size sheets. Your child will know exactly what time he is allowed to park himself in bed every night and when to wake up.

7:30 AM
TO 7:30 PM

No Parking

DUVET COVER

Finished cover: APPROXIMATELY 68½″ × 90½″

Materials

2 twin-size flat sheets for the background and backing

Approximately 36 strips 2½″ × 36" or longer, or 2½–2¾ yards, cut into 2½″-wide strips, of assorted reds for scrap appliqués and borders

7 strips 2½″ × at least 20″ long, or ¾–1 yard cut into 2½″-wide strips, of assorted blacks for scrap appliqués

2½ yards of fusible web

65″ length of Sullivans' Make-a-Zipper with 1 zipper pull*

Twin-size down or down-alternative comforter

*The zipper is the same length as the trimmed width of the flat sheet in Step 1 of Background (at right).

Background

All seams are ¼″ unless otherwise noted.

1. Trim the sheets to measure 3″ smaller each way than the size of the comforter, trimming off all the finished edges of the sheets in the process. (For example, if your comforter measures 68″ × 90″, your sheets should be trimmed to 65″ × 87″.)

2. Pin the closed zipper right side down along the right side of the bottom of a sheet, aligning the edges. Using the zipper foot on your sewing machine, stitch a side of the zipper in place.

3. Zigzag stitch or serge the raw edge to finish.

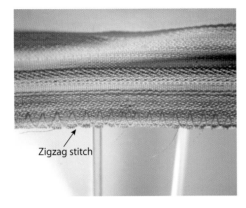

Zigzag stitch

One side of zipper stitched in place

4. Press the zigzag edge toward the sheet. Topstitch the zipper to the sheet.

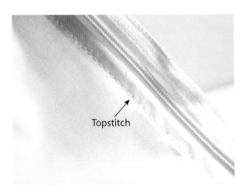

Topstitch

5. From the red strips, put enough aside for the scrap appliqué (18 strips 2½″ × 36″ will work for the appliqué). From the remaining red 2½″ strips, trim the strips to random lengths and sew the strips together end to end into the following measurements:

4 top and bottom border strips 2½″ × the width of the sheet + 1″ (66″ for the above example)

4 side border strips 2½″ × the length for the sheet + 4″ (91″ for the above example)

6. Press all the seam allowances in the same direction.

7. Stitch 2 of the shorter 2½" red pieced strips to the top and bottom of each sheet. For the sheet with the zipper, pin the red strip right side against the right side of the unattached zipper tape.

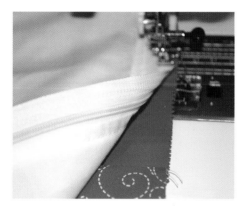

Note

The sheet with the zipper will become the bottom back side of your duvet cover.

8. Using your zipper foot, stitch the zipper in place on the red strip. Zigzag stitch or serge the raw edge to finish. Press the zigzag edge toward the red strip and topstitch. Trim the ends of the pieced red trim even with the sheet.

9. Stitch 2 of the longer 2½″ red pieced strips on the long sides of each sheet. Trim off the excess ends even with the sheet edge.

Scrap Appliqué

See Creating Scrap Appliqué (page 13) for detailed instructions. No Parking patterns are on pages 40–43 and pullout page 3, and they are reversed for fusible scrap appliqué.

1. Group the remaining colored 2½″ strips by color. Sew each color group of strips together to achieve approximately the following sizes:

Black: approximately 16″ × 19″

Red: approximately 36″ × 36″

2. Press all seam allowances in the same direction on both color sets.

Optional: Topstitch the seams down.

3. Enlarge the No Parking pullout pattern 200% and trace all the No Parking patterns onto the paper side of the fusible web.

4. Loosely cut around each of the fusible web templates. Position and iron the traced templates to the backside of the appropriate colored fabrics:

Black: C1

Red: C2 and 7:30 AM TO 7:30 PM (7-:-3-0-A-M-T-O-7-:-3-0-P-M)

5. Carefully cut out the fused templates on the traced lines, and remove the paper backing. Fuse the appliqués in place on your background fabric. (I centered the layout side to side and placed the top of the circle about 21″ down from the top edge.)

6. Machine appliqué the pieces with your favorite stitch type. I chose to do a small buttonhole stitch around all the pieces.

Finishing

1. With the zipper halfway open, match the front and back duvet pieces, right sides together.

2. Using a straight stitch and a ¼˝ seam allowance, stitch around all 4 sides of the duvet cover, and then use a zigzag stitch to finish the edges. (Or use a serger to stitch and finish in one step.)

3. Turn the duvet cover right side out through the zipper opening.

4. Insert the comforter.

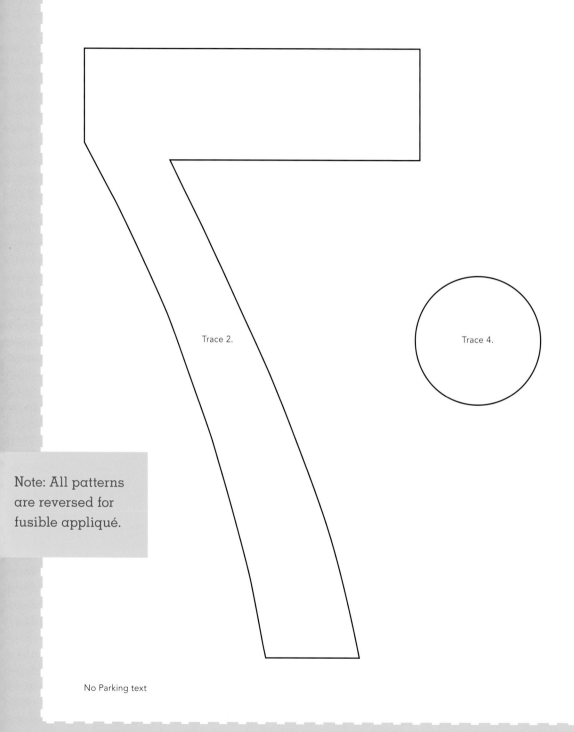

Trace 2.

Trace 4.

Note: All patterns are reversed for fusible appliqué.

No Parking text

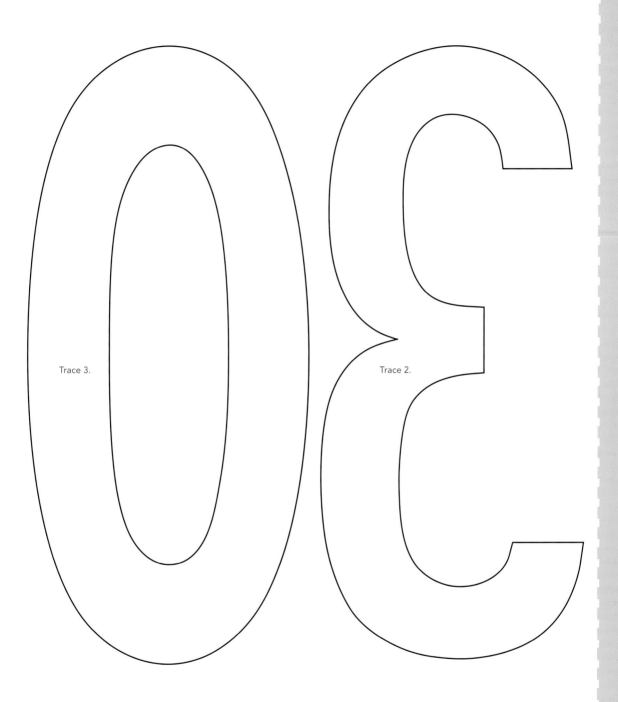

Trace 3.

Trace 2.

No Parking text, continued

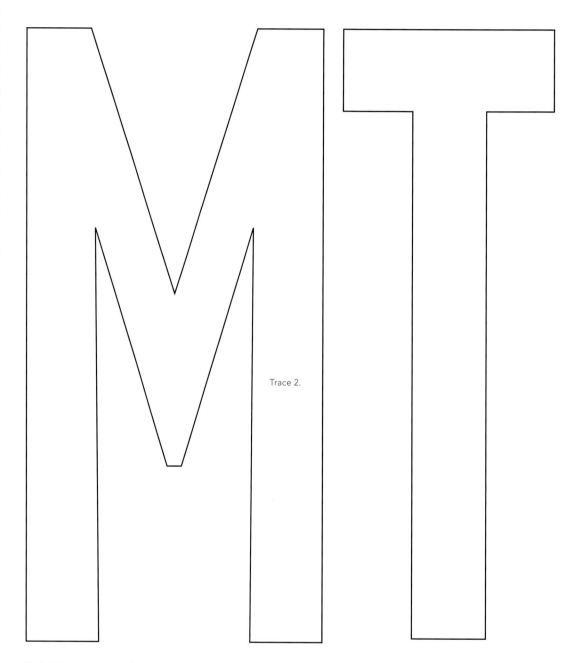

Trace 2.

No Parking text, continued

No Parking text, continued

No bed is complete without these fun road sign throw pillows—three basic shapes and sizes with appliqués of Speed Limit, No U-Turn, and Merge Traffic signs.

Road Signs
SPEED LIMIT PILLOW

Finished pillow:
APPROXIMATELY 13½″ × 17½″ without flange

Note: All seams allowances are ¼″ unless otherwise noted.

Materials

Assorted fabric scraps at least 18″ long in black and cream for the scrap appliqués, totaling about 1 fat quarter of each color

⅛ yard of black fabric for border

⅞ yard of coordinating fabric for pillow back and flange

½ yard of fusible web

Pillow form: 14″ × 18″ (Fairfield Soft Touch #ST1418)

Scrap Appliqué

See Creating Scrap Appliqué (page 13) for detailed instructions. The Speed Limit pattern is on pullout page P1 and is reversed for fusible scrap appliqué. Use the reverse appliqué method for this project (page 15).

1. Group the colored strips by color. Sew each color group of strips together to achieve approximately the following sizes:

   Black: 14˝ × 18˝

   Cream: 14˝ × 18˝

2. Press all the seam allowances in the same direction on each color set.

   Optional: Topstitch the seams down.

Note
This pillow uses the reverse appliqué method (see Creating Scrap Appliqué, pages 13–15).

3. Trace the entire Speed Limit pattern (including the outer line) onto the paper side of the fusible web.

4. Loosely cut around the outside of the fusible web template. Position and iron the traced template to the backside of the cream scrap-pieced fabric.

5. Carefully cut out the letters and numbers on the traced lines as indicated on the fused template from Step 4, and remove the paper backing from the surrounding cream pieced fabric.

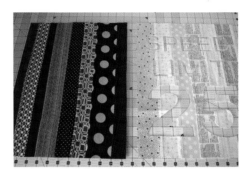

6. Fuse the cream appliqué on top of the black scrap-pieced fabric.

7. Machine appliqué the cream piece to the black piece around all of the openings with your favorite stitch. I chose a small buttonhole stitch.

8. Square and trim the pillow front to 12″ × 16″.

Finishing

1. From the black border fabric, cut 2 strips 1½″ × 14″ and 2 strips 1½″ × 16″.

2. Pin and stitch the 2 strips 1½″ × 16″ to the sides of the appliquéd pillow front. Press toward the border.

3. Pin and stitch the 2 strips 1½″ × 14″ to the top and bottom. Press toward the border.

4. From the flange fabric, cut 4 pieces 2½″ × 18″.

5. Pin and stitch 2 of the 18″ strips to the sides of the pillow front. Press toward the flange.

6. Pin and stitch the remaining 2 strips to the top and bottom of the pillow front. Press toward the flange.

7. From the pillow back fabric, cut 2 pieces 18″ × 16″.

8. On a piece of the pillow back, fold a long side under 1″, fold under 1″ again, and press. Topstitch along both sides of the folds to create a hem. Repeat for one long side of the other pillow back piece.

9. With the pillow front right side up, match the long raw edges of a back piece, right side down, at the top of the pillow front. Lay the second back piece right side down at the bottom of the pillow front, matching the long raw edges. The 2 hems of the backside should overlap, creating an opening to insert the pillow form. Pin and stitch around the 4 raw edges.

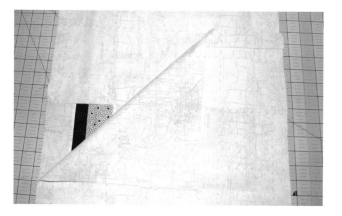

 TIP Remember to always backstitch when you begin and end a seam.

10. Turn the pillow right side out and press.

11. Topstitch on the flange, ⅛″ from the black border.

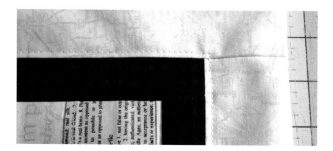

12. Insert the pillow form.

Road Signs
MERGE TRAFFIC PILLOW

Finished pillow:
APPROXIMATELY 15½″ × 15½″

Materials

Strips of assorted fabric scraps in yellow and black for the scrap appliqués and base, totaling about 1 fat quarter of each color

⅝ yard of black fabric for pillow borders and back

⅜ yard of fusible web

Pillow form: 16″ × 16″ square (Fairfield Home Elegance #XP16S)

14″ black zipper (YKK Ziplon Coil Zipper 14″ 580 black)

Scrap Appliqué

See Creating Scrap Appliqué (page 13) for detailed instructions. The Merge Traffic pattern is on pullout page P2 and is reversed for fusible scrap appliqué.

1. Group the colored strips by color. Sew each color group of strips together to achieve approximately the following sizes:

   Black: 12″ × 12″

   Yellow: 16″ × 16″

2. Press all the seam allowances in the same direction on each color set.

   Optional: Topstitch the seams down.

3. Trace the Merge Traffic pattern onto the paper side of the fusible web.

4. Loosely cut around the fusible web template. Position and iron the traced template to the backside of the black pieced fabric.

5. Carefully cut out the fused template on the traced lines, and remove the paper backing.

6. Position and fuse the black appliqué on top of the yellow pieced fabric.

7. Machine appliqué the black piece to the yellow piece with your favorite stitch. I chose a small buttonhole stitch.

8. Square and trim the yellow piece to 15″ × 15″.

Finishing

1. From the black pillow back fabric, cut 2 strips 1″ × 15″ and 2 strips 1″ × 16″.

2. Pin and stitch the 2 strips 1″ × 15″ to the sides of the pillow front.

3. Pin and stitch the 2 strips 1″ × 16″ to the top and bottom of the pillow front to create a border.

4. Pin the zipper right side down, centered on the right side bottom edge of the pillow front. Using the zipper foot, stitch the zipper in place. Press the seam allowances toward the wrong side of the pillow front and topstitch.

5. From the black pillow back fabric, cut a piece 16″ × 16″.

6. Lay the pillow front right side up, and place the pillow back right side down on top of it. Line up the raw edge of the zipper tape with the raw edge of the backing fabric, pin, and stitch in place using the zipper foot. Press the seam allowances toward the wrong side of the backing fabric and topstitch.

7. Unzip the zipper about halfway. Match the pillow front and back, right sides together, pin, and stitch along the 3 raw-edge sides. On the side with the zipper, stitch just on the very ends of the pillow to close up the edges that the zipper does not cover. Do not stitch the zipper closed.

Optional: Zigzag or serge the 3 raw edges.

8. Turn the pillow right side out through the zipper opening. Insert pillow form and zip the pillow closed.

Road Signs
NO U-TURN PILLOW

Finished pillow:
APPROXIMATELY 13¾˝ round

Materials

About 8–15 strips of assorted fabric scraps in red at least 16˝ long for the scrap appliqué

About 5–10 strips of assorted fabric scraps in black at least 11˝ long for the scrap appliqué

Fat quarter or 16˝ × 16˝ of cream for pillow base

Fat quarter or 16˝ × 16˝ of black for pillow back

¾ yard of fusible web

Pillow form: 14˝ round (Fairfield Soft Touch #STR14)

Scrap Appliqué

See Creating Scrap Appliqué (page 13) for detailed instructions. The No U-Turn pattern components are on pullout pages P1 and P2, and they are reversed for fusible scrap appliqué.

1. Group the colored 2½˝ strips by color. Sew each color group of strips together to achieve approximately the following sizes:

   Black: 10˝ × 10˝

   Red: 15˝ × 15˝

2. Press all the seams in the same direction on each color set.

    Optional: Topstitch the seams down.

3. Trace the No U-Turn patterns (pullout pages P1 and P2) onto the paper side of the fusible web.

4. Loosely cut around each of the fusible web templates. Position and iron the traced templates to the backside of the appropriate colored fabrics:

    Black: D4

    Red: D3

5. Carefully cut out the fused templates on the traced lines, and remove the paper backing.

6. Position and fuse the appliqués in place on the piece of coordinating cream fabric. Trim the cream fabric down to ⅛˝ larger than the red circle.

7. Machine appliqué around the appliqués with your favorite stitch. I chose a small buttonhole stitch. Be sure to skip the overlapping areas where needed so that you get a nice, clean appliquéd finish.

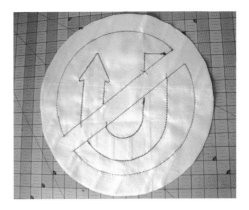

Finishing

1. Cut the black pillow back fabric to the same size as the pillow front. Place the pillow front and back right sides together, pin, and stitch with a ¼˝ seam allowance, leaving a 6˝–8˝ opening for turning and stuffing.

2. Turn the pillow right side out and insert the pillow form.

3. Hand stitch the opening closed.

This fabric wall art is sure to make visitors stop in their tracks to admire the simple fusion of fabric and art.

Stop
WALL ART

Finished wall art: 30″ × 30″

Materials

15 strips in solid red (2½″ × width of fabric)

34″ × 34″ square of natural muslin

Strips of assorted fabric scraps at least 11″ long, or approximately ½ yard, of cream fabric for the scrap appliqué

2½ yards of fusible web

34″ × 34″ square of fusible fleece

4 wooden canvas stretcher bars 30″ long

Staple gun and staples

Base

All seams are ¼″ unless otherwise noted.

1. Sew the 15 red strips together, creating a base fabric for your appliqués.

STRAIGHT STRIPS

When sewing the 2½″ strips together, make sure they match up end to end so you don't get a curve in the finished piece. Match the ends together, stitch about ½″, and then stop. Make sure the needle is in the down position, and then pull the strips so that the center folds match on each strip. Hold the strips together while sewing to these folds. With the needle in the down position, pull the strips again so that the bottoms of the strips match up. Hold in place while you finish sewing to the bottoms of the strips. Alternate the ends where you start stitching, and repeat for each strip.

2. Press all the seam allowances in the same direction. Topstitch ⅛″ from each seam.

3. Cover a 31″ × 31″ area of the wrong side of the red pieced strips with fusible web.

4. Trim the area from Step 3 to 30″ × 30″.

5. Place a rotary ruler across a corner at a 45° angle, 9″ down and 9″ across. Cut off the corner.

6. Repeat Step 5 to trim off all 4 corners.

7. Remove the paper backing and fuse the stop sign to the center of the muslin fabric.

8. Topstitch ⅛″ and ⅜″ from the raw edges of the stop sign.

Scrap Appliqué

See Creating Scrap Appliqué (page 13) for detailed instructions. Patterns are on pullout pages P2 and P3 and are reversed for fusible scrap appliqué.

1. Sew the cream strips together to create a 26″ × 11″ piece.

2. Press all the seam allowances in the same direction.

   Optional: Topstitch the seams down.

3. Trace the patterns for the letters S–T–O–P onto the paper side of the fusible web.

4. Loosely cut around each of the fusible web templates. Position and iron the traced templates to the backside of the cream fabric.

5. Carefully cut out the fused templates on the traced lines, and remove the paper backing. Fuse the appliqués in place on the red pieced base fabric.

6. Machine appliqué around the letters with your favorite stitch. I chose to do a straight stitch ⅛″ around all the pieces to allow the edges to fray.

Finishing

1. Fuse the fleece to the wrong side of the muslin.

2. Assemble the canvas stretcher bars by inserting one end into the next, creating a big square. Staple the corners in place to prevent any shifting.

3. Place the appliquéd fabric piece facedown. Center the wooden frame on the fabric.

4. Carefully stretch the fabric over the edges of the frame and staple to the backside. Continue to staple until you have all the edges and corners secured to the back.

Sto

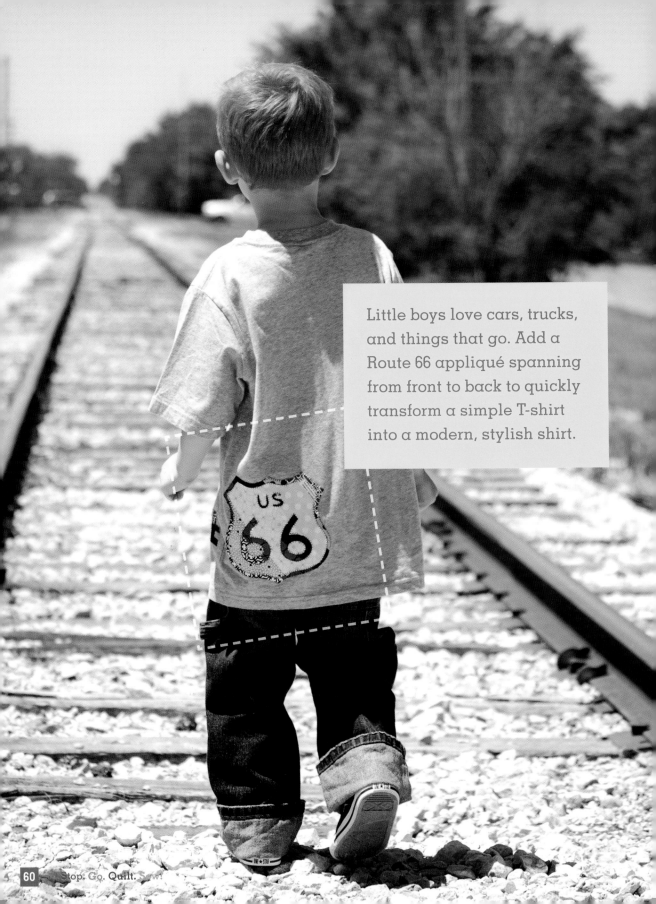

Little boys love cars, trucks, and things that go. Add a Route 66 appliqué spanning from front to back to quickly transform a simple T-shirt into a modern, stylish shirt.

Route 66
T-SHIRT

Photo by Angela Yosten

Materials

T-shirt

Strips of assorted fabric scraps, or approximately ½ yard of fabric, in coordinating blacks for the scrap appliqués

Strips of assorted fabric scraps, or approximately ¼ yard of fabric, in coordinating creams for the scrap appliqués

½ yard of fusible web

Scrap Appliqué

See Creating Scrap Appliqué (page 13) for detailed instructions. The Route 66 patterns are on pages 64 and 65 and are reversed for fusible scrap appliqué. The letters R–O–U–T–E are appliquéd directly onto the shirt front; the US 66 sign is added on the shirt back using the reverse appliqué method (page 15).

1. Group the colored strips by color. Sew each color group of strips together to achieve approximately the following sizes:

   Black: 8″ × 8″ and 3″ × 10″

   Cream: 8″ × 8″

2. Press all the seam allowances in the same direction on each color set.

Topstitch the seams down.

3. Trace the Route 66 patterns onto the paper side of the fusible web. (Trace the outer sign outline of F1 and the R-O-U-T-E patterns for the black fabric; trace the inner outline and text of F1 for the cream fabric. The letters and numbers of the cream fabric are cut away using the reverse appliqué method and then reveal the black layer when it is fused underneath.)

4. Loosely cut around each of the fusible web templates. Position and iron the traced templates to the backside of the appropriate colored fabrics.

   Black: F1

   Trace and cut around only the outside line of the sign and the letters R-O-U-T-E.

   Cream: F1

   Trace and cut around the inside line of the sign and the text US 66 (reverse appliqué style).

5. Fuse the cream appliqué on top of the black base. When the cream sign is layered on the black sign, the black letters and surround should show through the cream. Fuse all the appliqués in place on the T-shirt.

6. Machine appliqué around the pieces with your favorite stitch. I chose a small buttonhole stitch.

Front of shirt

Back of shirt

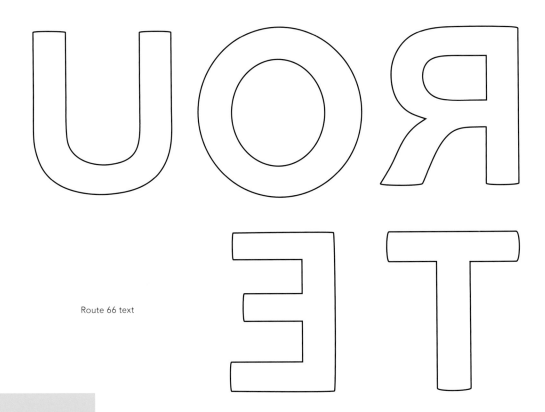

Route 66 text

Note: All patterns are reversed for fusible appliqué.

Route 66
F1
Make 2.

Route 66 sign

Keep intruders out of your bag with this warning sign. With its many pockets, you are sure to be able to find a place for everything.

Materials

1¾ yards of corduroy or home decor–weight exterior fabric

1½ yards of interior lining fabric

Strips of assorted fabric scraps at least 16″ long, or ½ yard total of fabric, in coordinating reds for the scrap appliqué base

Strips of assorted fabric scraps at least 16″ long, or ⅛ yard total of fabric, in coordinating creams for the scrap appliqué

¼ yard of fusible web

¼ yard of double-sided stiff fusible interfacing (fast2fuse heavyweight interfacing)

1 yard of fusible fleece

2 yards of soft fusible interfacing (4 craft packs of Shape-Flex interfacing)

Fabric pencil (Sewline)

14″ black coil zipper (YKK Ziplon Coil Zipper 14″ 580 black)

¾″ magnetic snap (Dritz #763-65)

⅞″ metal D-ring swivel hook (Dritz #123)

2 strap adjusters, 1″ (Dritz #477)

1″ × 60″ nylon strapping (Dritz #478)

Do Not Enter
MESSENGER BAG

Finished bag:
APPROXIMATELY 14″ wide × 12¼″ high × 4″ deep

FROM THE EXTERIOR FABRIC, CUT:

2 pieces 15″ × 13″ (front and back main panels)

2 pieces 5″ × 13″ (side panels)

2 pieces 5″ × 7½″ (exterior side pockets)

1 piece 15″ × 5″ (bottom panel)

1 piece 15″ × 15″ (flap lining)

1 piece 3″ × 3″ (keychain tab)

1 piece 14¾″ × 20″ (inside large pocket)

1 piece 14¾″ × 17″ (inside medium pocket)

FROM THE LINING FABRIC, CUT:

2 pieces 15″ × 13″ (exterior back pocket)

2 pieces 5″ × 7½″ (exterior side pockets)

2 pieces 14¾″ × 12¾″ (front and back main panels)

2 pieces 4¾″ × 12¾″ (side panels)

1 piece 14¾″ × 4¾″ (bottom panel)

1 piece 14¾″ × 13″ (inside small pocket)

FROM THE FUSIBLE FLEECE, CUT:

2 pieces 14¾″ × 12¾″
(front and back lining panels)

2 pieces 4¾″ × 12¾″ (side lining panels)

FROM THE SHAPE-FLEX, CUT:

4 pieces 15″ × 13″ (front and back panels and exterior back pocket layers)

2 pieces 5″ × 13″ (side panels)

4 pieces 5″ × 7½″
(exterior side pockets)

2 pieces 15″ × 15″ (exterior flap and exterior flap lining)

2 pieces 15″ × 5″
(exterior bottom panel)

1 piece 3″ × 3″ (keychain tab)

1 piece 14¾″ × 4¾″
(lining bottom panel)

1 piece 14¾″ × 13″ (inside small pocket)

1 piece 14¾″ × 20″ (inside large pocket)

1 piece 14¾″ × 17″
(inside medium pocket)

FROM THE FAST2FUSE, CUT:

1 piece 14″ × 4″ (bottom panel)

Scrap Appliqué

All seam allowances are ¼″ to create the scrap appliqué unless otherwise noted. See Creating Scrap Appliqué (page 13) for detailed instructions. Do Not Enter patterns are on page 81. The patterns are reversed for fusible scrap appliqué.

1. Group the colored strips by color. Sew each color group of strips together to achieve approximately the following sizes for the flap:

   Red: 16″ × 10″ (top section), 16″ × 4½″ (bottom section)

   Cream: 16″ × 3¾″ (middle section), 16″ × 8″ (letters)

Note that the fabric strips run parallel to the long dimension of the flap.

2. Press the seams all the same direction on each color set.

   Optional: Topstitch the seams down.

3. Trim the top red section to 15″ × 9″, the middle cream section to 15″ × 2¾″, and the bottom red section to 15″ × 4¼″.

4. Stitch the top section to the middle section, right sides together. Then stitch the middle section to the bottom section. Press. The finished size should be 15″ × 15″. This becomes the flap of the bag.

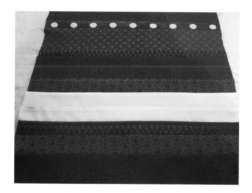

5. Trace the lettering patterns onto the paper side of the fusible web.

6. Loosely cut around each of the fusible web templates. Position and iron the traced templates to the backside of the cream 16″ × 8″ piece of scrap-pieced fabric. I placed the letters so the stripes of the appliqué letters run horizontally.

7. Carefully cut out the fused templates on the traced lines, and remove the paper backing.

8. Fuse the appliqués in place on the bag flap above and below the center cream strip. The letters should be placed about ¾″ above and below the center strip.

9. Machine appliqué the letters to your base fabric with your favorite stitch type. I chose to do a small buttonhole stitch around all the pieces to complete the front of the flap.

Attach Interfacings

1. Fuse the fusible side of the fleece to the wrong side of the lining front, back, and side panels (4 pieces total) using the iron's wool setting.

2. Fuse the Shape-Flex interfacing to the wrong side of all the remaining pieces (including the pieced flap), matching the sizes. (A piece of Shape-Flex is left for Step 4.)

3. Center the fast2fuse on the wrong side of the exterior bottom panel.

4. Place the remaining Shape-Flex interfacing bottom panel piece (15″ × 5″), fusible side down, to sandwich the fast2fuse in the unit from Step 3. Press into place.

Assembly

All seam allowances are ½″ unless otherwise noted.

Interior Pockets

1. With the wrong sides together, fold the inside large pocket in half (14¾″ × 10″). Press and topstitch ¼″ and ⅜″ from the fold for a double-stitched look.

2. Repeat Step 1 for the inside medium pocket (14¾″ × 8½″) and inside small pocket (14¾″ × 6½″).

3. Place a lining/main panel piece with the lining side up.

4. Fold the large pocket piece in half vertically to find the center. Place the large pocket on top of the lining/main panel, matching the bottoms and sides, and stitch down the center fold. Be sure to backstitch at the top of the pocket.

5. Repeat Step 4 for the small pocket.

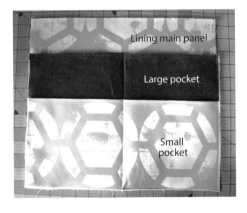

6. On the small pocket, draw lines with a fabric pencil, 2¼″ and 4½″ to the left of the center stitching.

7. Fold the lining main panel away from the pockets on the left.

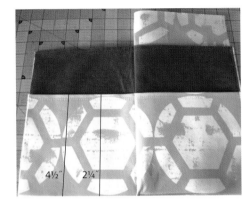

8. Stitch the small pocket to the large pocket on the drawn lines.

9. Unfold the lining main panel back into position and stitch ⅛″ inside the edges around the sides and bottom, through all layers, to secure the pockets.

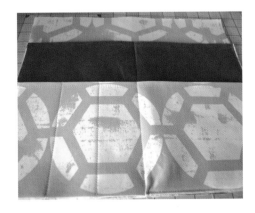

10. Place the other lining/main panel with the lining side up. Place the medium pocket on top, matching the raw edges at the bottom and sides. Stitch around the sides and bottom ⅛″ from the edge to secure the pocket.

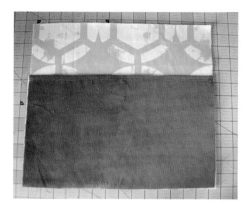

Keychain Tab

1. Fold the keychain tab fabric in half, right sides together. Stitch with a ¼″ seam allowance along the long raw edges. Leave open the 2 short ends. Turn right side out using a bodkin or turning tool. Press with the seam centered.

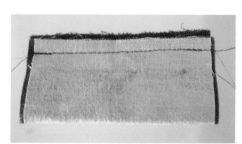

2. Topstitch ¼″ from each folded side.

3. Slip the end of the keychain tab through the D-ring of the swivel hook. Place a lining/side panel with the lining right side up. Center and match the raw edges of the fabric of the keychain tab to the top of the side panel. Stitch ⅛″ from the edge to hold the keychain tab in place.

Assembling the Interior

1. Place a lining main panel and a lining side panel with right sides together. Pin the side edges. Stitch with a ½″ seam allowance, stopping ½″ from the bottom edge. Backstitch. Press. Repeat to add the other lining side panel.

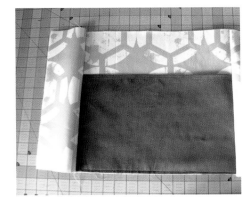

2. Repeat Step 1 to attach the second main lining panel to the opposite side of the lining side panels.

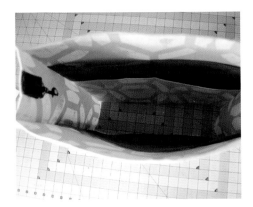

3. Place the bottom edges of the lining main panels and the long edge of the lining bottom panel, right sides together. Pin along both sides. Stitch with a ½˝ seam allowance, starting and stopping ½˝ from each end. Backstitch at each end.

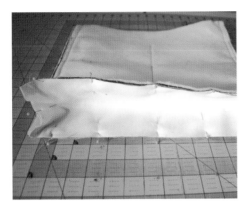

4. Similarly, match the short sides and pin. Stitch with a ½˝ seam allowance along each side, and then backstitch at each end.

5. Carefully trim the seam allowances to ¼˝ on all sides of the bag. This will help reduce the bulk of the seam allowances. Leave the lining wrong side out.

Exterior Zipper Pocket

1. Place an exterior back pocket from lining fabric right side up. Place the zipper right side up along the 15˝ side. Place the exterior back main panel on top of the lining and zipper, with right sides together, matching the raw edges.

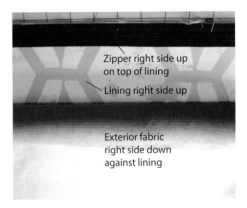

Zipper right side up on top of lining

Lining right side up

Exterior fabric right side down against lining

2. Using a zipper foot, stitch the zipper, sandwiched between the 2 fabrics, so the stitching is on the outer tape of the zipper. Leave enough room for the zipper pull to slide smoothly.

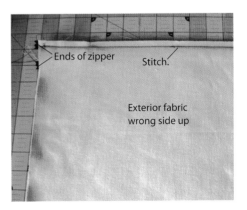

Ends of zipper

Stitch.

Exterior fabric wrong side up

3. Open the seam and press the fabrics, wrong sides together, with the zipper out.

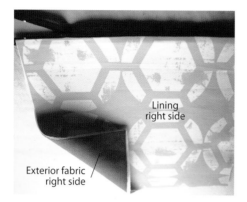

Lining right side

Exterior fabric right side

4. Place the flap lining (cut from the exterior fabric) right side up. Determine which side is the bottom of the flap. Following the manufacturer's directions, attach the upper portion of the snap 1½˝ from the bottom and centered on the flap lining.

5. Place the 2 flap units (pieced flap and flap lining) right sides together. Be sure the tops and bottoms line up.

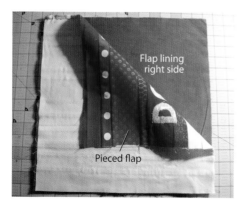

Flap lining right side

Pieced flap

6. Stitch along the sides and bottom with a ½˝ seam allowance. Carefully clip the corners and turn the flap right side out through the top. Topstitch ¼˝ from the edge, around the sides and bottom of the flap.

7. Place the second exterior back pocket from lining fabric right side up. Place the first exterior back pocket (from Step 3) on top, right sides of lining layers together, aligning the raw edge of the zipper along the top. (At this point, the right side of the exterior main panel faces up. Keep the zipper closed, and it also faces up.) Center the flap front with the appliqué side facedown, matching the raw edges. Pin in place.

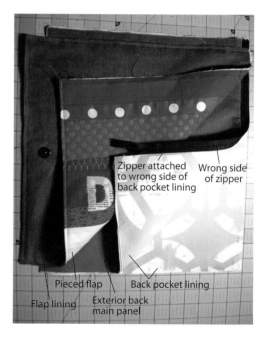

Zipper attached to wrong side of back pocket lining

Wrong side of zipper

Pieced flap

Back pocket lining

Flap lining

Exterior back main panel

8. Using a zipper foot, stitch through all the layers with a ¼″ seam allowance. Open and test the zipper.

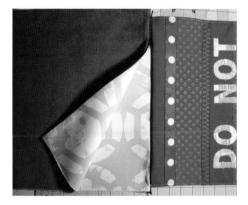

Exterior Pockets

1. Place 2 exterior side pocket pieces 5″ × 7½″ right sides together, a piece from the lining fabric and a piece from the exterior fabric. Stitch with a ½″ seam allowance along a 5″ side and press the seams open.

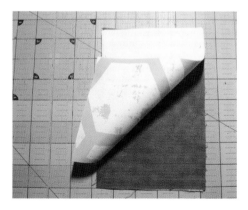

2. Place the pieces from Step 1 wrong sides together and press. Turn the seam edge over to the exterior fabric side 1″ and topstitch ⅛″ and ¼″ from the seam through all the layers.

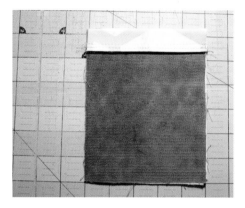

3. Repeat Steps 1 and 2 for the second exterior side pocket.

4. Place the exterior side panels right sides up. Place the side pockets with the exterior fabric facing up, matching the bottom raw edge and the lower side edges. Stitch ⅛″ inside the bottom and sides to hold in place.

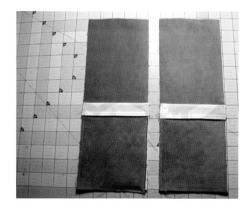

Assembling the Exterior

1. Place an exterior side panel right sides together with the back main panel. Fold the flap out of the way so that you do not stitch it in the seam. Pin and stitch with a ½˝ seam allowance.

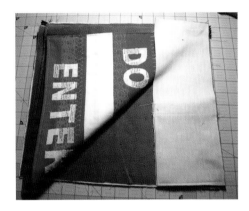

2. Repeat Step 1 to attach the other side panel.

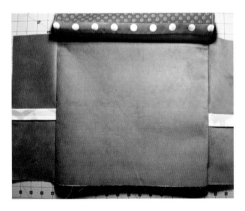

3. Place the exterior front panel (15˝ × 13˝) facing up. Determine which side is the bottom of the panel. Following the manufacturer's directions, attach the lower portion of the snap 4½˝ from the bottom and centered on the panel.

4. Repeat Steps 1 and 2 to attach the front main exterior panel to the bag.

5. Place the bottom edges of the exterior main panels and the long edge of the exterior bottom panel right sides together. Pin along both sides. Stitch with a ½˝ seam allowance, starting and stopping ½˝ from either end. Backstitch.

6. Similarly, match the short sides and pin. Stitch with a ½˝ seam allowance along each side.

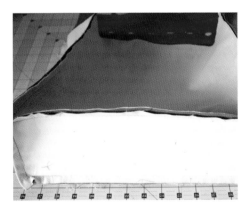

7. Carefully, trim ther seam allowances to
¼″ on all sides of the bag.

8. Turn the bag right side out.

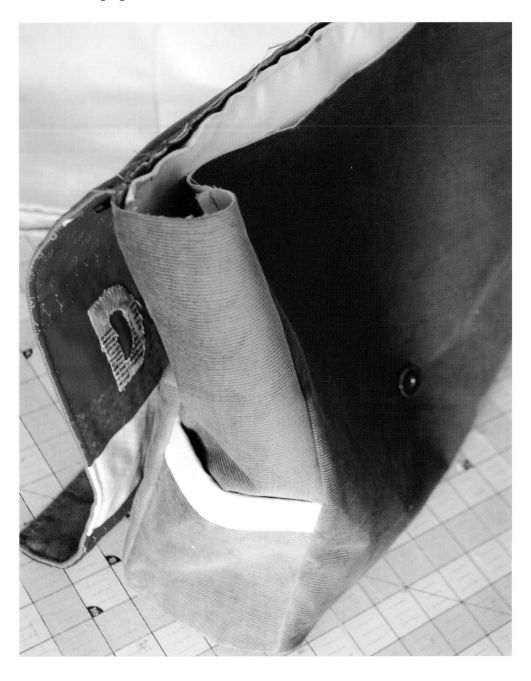

Finishing

1. From the nylon strap, cut a 5″ piece. Slip the end through the strap adjuster following the directions on the package. Match the raw ends and stitch ⅛″ from the raw edges.

>
>
> **TIP**
>
> To help prevent the nylon strap from fraying at the cut ends, use a lighter to melt the ends just slightly.

2. To help reinforce the strap, stitch a large X just under the strap adjuster.

3. Center the strap adjuster on a side panel (on the right side) of the exterior bag and pin in place with the strap pointing down. Stitch with a ⅛″ seam allowance to hold the strap adjuster in place.

4. On the opposite side of the exterior bag, attach the remaining length of nylon strap at the same location as the keychain tab. Remember to match the nylon raw end with the raw edges at the top of the bag.

5. Place the exterior bag inside the lining bag, right sides together. Pin raw edges together.

6. Stitch with a ¼″ seam allowance along the top of the bag, leaving a 6″ opening on the front edge of the bag for turning. When stitching the backside of the bag, stitch in the same location as the zipper stitching. This will help the zipper slide nicely.

7. Turn the bag right side out through the 6″ opening. Press along this seam. Topstitch along the sides and the front of the bag. Do not topstitch the backside of the bag by the zipper. The swivel hook should be topstitched pointing down, while the nylon straps should be topstitched pointing up.

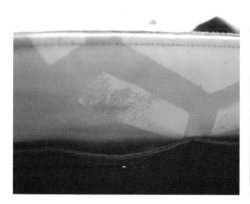 

8. Slip the long strap through the 2 strap adjusters, following the manufacturer's directions.

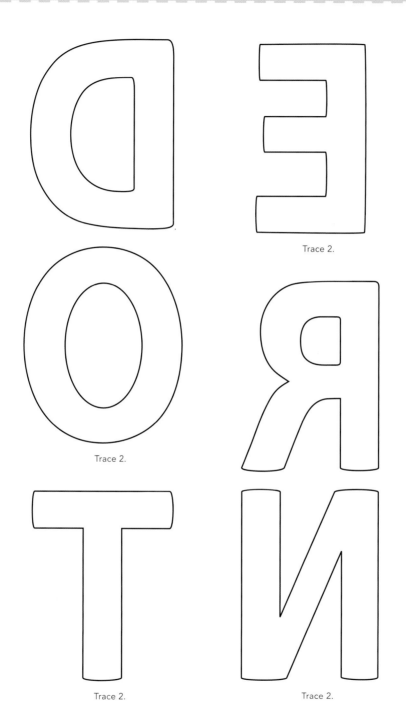

Trace 2.

Trace 2.

Trace 2.

Trace 2.

Trace 2.

Do Not Enter text

Note: All patterns are reversed for fusible appliqué.

Every kid will want to see if he can spot a kangaroo while sporting his new Roo jacket. Add a simple Roo Crossing sign to the back of any jacket or hoodie to achieve an adorable look.

Roo Crossing
HOODIE OR JACKET

Photo by Angela Yosten

Materials

Jacket or hoodie

Strips of assorted fabric scraps about 7″ long, or approximately ¼ yard total of fabric, in coordinating blacks

Strips of assorted fabric scraps about 7″ long, or approximately ¼ yard total of fabric, in coordinating yellows

½ yard of fusible web

Scrap Appliqué

See Creating Scrap Appliqué (page 13) for detailed instructions. The Roo Crossing pattern is on page 85 and is reversed for fusible scrap appliqué. Use the reverse appliqué method (page 15) for this project.

1. Group the colored strips by color. Sew each color group of strips together to achieve approximately the following sizes:

   Black: 7″ × 7″

   Yellow: 7″ × 7″

2. Press all the seam allowances in the same direction on each color set.

   Optional: Topstitch the seams down.

3. Trace the Roo Crossing patterns onto the paper side of the fusible web. Trace the outer sign outline of H1 for the black fabric and trace the inner outline and kangaroo for the yellow fabric.

4. Loosely cut around each of the fusible web templates. Position and iron the traced templates to the back of the appropriate colored fabrics.

Black: H1

Trace and cut around only the outside line of the sign.

Yellow: H1

Trace and cut around the inside line of the sign and the kangaroo (reverse appliqué style).

Note

When the yellow sign is layered on the black sign, the black kangaroo and surround should show through the yellow.

5. Fuse the yellow appliqué on top of the black base. (I placed the strips facing in opposite directions for a pleasing effect.)

6. Fuse the appliqués in place on the back of the jacket.

7. Machine appliqué around the pieces with your favorite stitch. I chose a small buttonhole stitch.

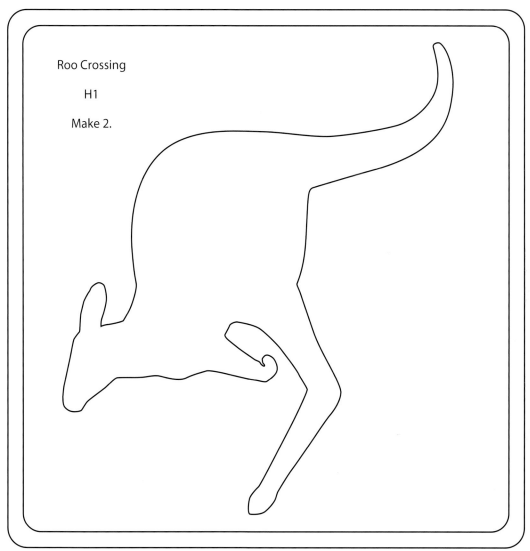

Roo Crossing

H1

Make 2.

Roo Crossing

Note: The pattern is reversed for fusible appliqué.

Kids will want to cuddle up in this quilted nap sack every night. It's great for naptime and sleepovers.

Materials

4 yards of corduroy

5½ yards of lining fabric

¾ yard accent fabric for pillow

Strips of assorted fabric scraps, or approximately 2 yards total of fabric, in coordinating blacks at least 27″ long for scrap appliqué

4 yards of fusible web

2 center release buckles, 1″ (Dritz #475)

36″ × 68″ of quilt batting

12″ × 16″ pillow form

Long ruler with marked 60° angle

Slow
NAP SACK

Finished nap sack: APPROXIMATELY 32″ × 64″
Photo by Angela Yosten

FROM THE CORDUROY FABRIC, CUT:

1 piece 32″ × 46″ for sack front

1 piece 32″ × 64″ for sack back

1 piece 16″ × 12″ for pillow

FROM LINING FABRIC, CUT:

2 pieces each 72″ x width of fabric for backing (An extra 18″ is included to make matching the front and lining fabrics easier when assembling for quilting.)

8 strips 2½″ × width of fabric for appliqué

7 strips 2½″ × width of fabric for binding

4 strips 2½″ × 15″ for the straps

FROM PILLOW ACCENT FABRIC, CUT:

1 piece 20″ × 18″ for pillow back

1 strip 2½″ × 20″ for pillow border

2 strips 2½″ × 12″ for pillow border

1 strip 3½″ × 40″ for pillow border

Scrap Appliqué

All seams are ¼˝ unless otherwise noted. See Creating Scrap Appliqué (page 13) for detailed instructions. Letter patterns are on page 95. They are reversed for fusible scrap appliqué.

1. From the black scraps, sew strips together to create 4 strip sets approximately 11˝ × 26˝.

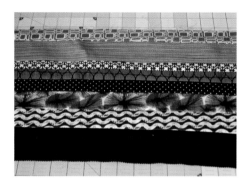

2. Take the 8 strips of lining fabric and press each in half lengthwise, with wrong sides together.

3. Place a folded strip from Step 2 along the length of a black strip set, right sides together, matching the raw edges. Pin and stitch. Repeat this step to add a lining strip to each side of each black strip set. Trim the folded strips even with the ends of the black strips.

4. Press the seams all the same direction.

   Optional: Topstitch the seams down.

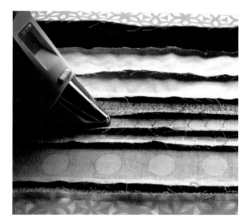

5. Place 2 strip sets right sides together.

6. Starting at a corner, make a 60° cut through both strip sets with a rotary cutter. Discard the cut triangles.

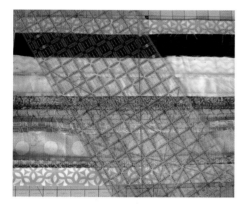

7. Stitch through both layers with a ¼″ seam allowance along the angled cut. Press the seam open.

8. Repeat Steps 5–7 for the remaining 2 strip sets.

9. Fuse the fusible web to the wrong side of the chevron-shaped units. Remove the paper backing.

10. Fold the 32″ × 46″ corduroy in half lengthwise to find the center. Center the 2 chevron appliqués from Step 9 approximately 5″ apart. Press the chevrons in place to fuse to the corduroy.

11. Trim the excess fabric from the ends of the 2 chevrons.

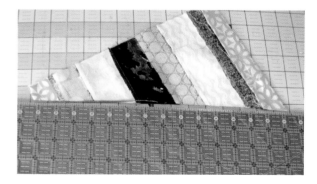

Quilting

1. Place the large piece of corduroy and the appliquéd corduroy right sides together, matching the bottom edges. Stitch with a ¼″ seam allowance along a side. Press the seam open.

2. Place the 2 large pieces of lining right sides together, matching the selvages. Stitch with a ½″ seam allowance along a side. Press the seam open.

3. Sandwich the lining, batting, and quilt top together and safety pin baste through all the layers.

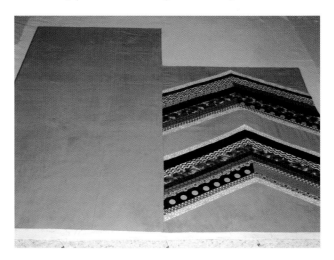

4. Machine quilt as desired.

5. Trim away any excess lining fabric and batting on all sides to square up and match the exterior side of the nap sack.

Pillow

1. Stitch the 2 strips 2½″ × 12″ of pillow accent fabric to the short sides of the corduroy pillow fabric. Press.

2. Stitch the 2½˝ × 20˝ strip of pillow accent fabric to the bottom of the pillow. Press.

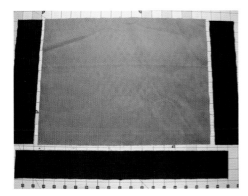

3. Match the short ends of the 3½˝ × 40˝ strip, right sides together, and stitch a ¼˝ seam allowance. Turn right side out. Press flat with the seam at an end.

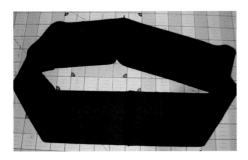

4. Matching raw edges, stitch the 3½˝ double-thickness strip to the top of the pillow front, centering the strip. Zigzag or serge this raw seam edge. Press the seam allowance toward the 3½˝ strip and topstitch with a ⅛˝ seam.

5. Trace the patterns for the letters s–l–o–w onto the paper side of the fusible web.

6. Loosely cut around each of the fusible web templates. Position and iron the traced templates to the backside of the lining fabric.

7. Carefully cut out the fused templates on the traced lines, and remove the paper backing. Fuse the appliqués in place on the front pillow corner.

8. Machine appliqué around the pieces with your favorite stitch. I chose a small buttonhole stitch.

9. Fold the top long edge of the pillow backing toward the wrong side of the fabric 1″ and press. Fold again 2″ and press. Stitch with a ⅛″ seam allowance along each side of the rolled hem.

10. Place the pillow front and back right sides together, matching the bottom and side raw edges. The tops will not be even. Stitch with a ¼″ seam allowance along the bottom and 2 sides. Do not stitch across the top. Clip the 2 lower corners and turn the pillow right side out. Press.

11. Topstitch ⅛″ from the pillow center to create a pillow flange.

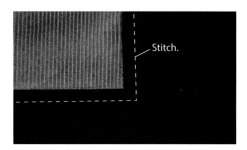

Finishing

1. Place the raw edge of the pillow top right side up, centered at the top of the nap sack on the lining. Pin and stitch in place using a ⅛″ seam allowance.

2. Bind all the edges of the nap sack. Be careful to sew only the top of the pillow when attaching the binding. Refer to Binding (page 16) for step-by-step instructions.

3. Fold each strap strip in half lengthwise, right sides together, and stitch with a ¼″ seam allowance down the long side.

4. Using a bodkin or turning tool, turn the tubes right side out. Press with the seam on one side.

5. Fold and press an end under ¼˝. Weave the folded end through one side of the buckle. Fold over itself 1˝, hiding the ¼˝ hem. Stitch in place. Repeat this step with the second strip on the opposite end of the buckle.

6. Repeat Step 5 for the other set of straps and buckle.

7. Fold the nap sack exterior sides together so that the bottom and side edges match. Pin the nap sack along the bottom and about halfway up one front side. (Remember, the front side is shorter than the back.)

8. Release the buckle so that you have 2 separate pieces for each buckle. With each set of straps right sides together, pin the strap raw edges between the 2 layers of the nap sack creating a "sandwich." Each set of straps should be approximately 8˝ from each side of the nap sack along the bottom. The loose raw ends of the straps should be hidden inside the nap sack.

9. Starting at the bottom folded corner, stitch with a ½˝ seam allowance across the bottom, pivot at the corner, and stitch up the side to the last pin, which should be only halfway up the front side. With the needle in the down position, turn the foot so it angles off the end of the nap sack to finish the seam. Backstitch this angle a few times to reinforce the end.

10. Turn the nap sack right side out to reveal the straps and cool new nap sack.

11. Insert the pillow form in the opening on the back. Starting at the pillow, roll up the nap sack, until you reach the end by the straps. Snap the buckles closed, and it's ready to carry.

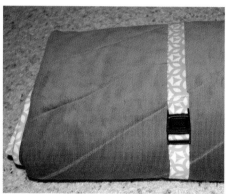

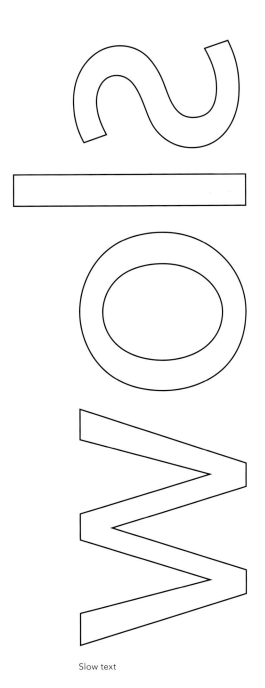

Slow text

Note: All patterns are reversed for fusible appliqué.

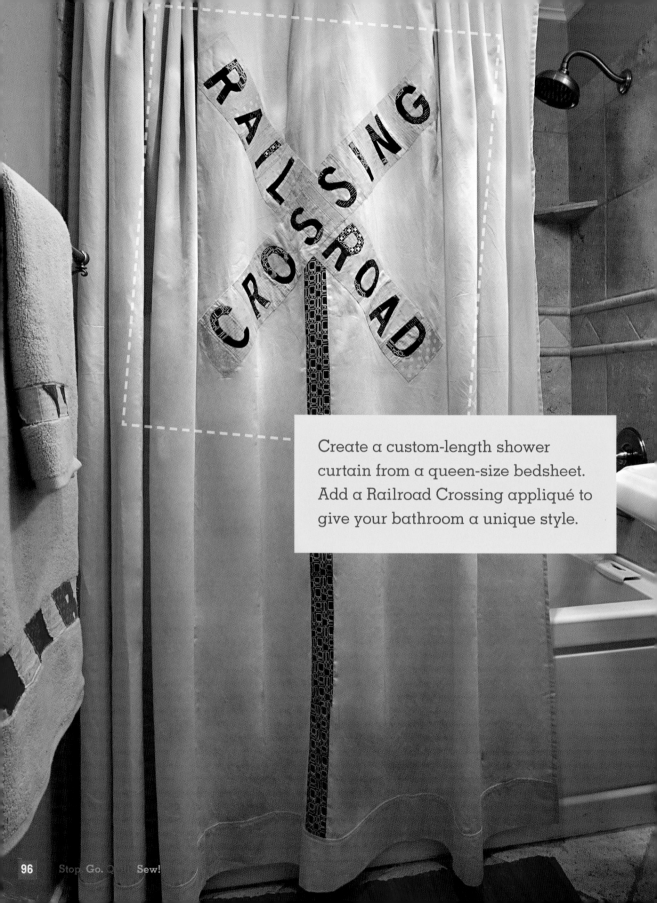

Create a custom-length shower curtain from a queen-size bedsheet. Add a Railroad Crossing appliqué to give your bathroom a unique style.

Railroad Crossing
SHOWER CURTAIN

Materials

Queen-size flat sheet

Strips of assorted fabric scraps, or approximately 1 yard of fabric, in coordinating creams for the scrap appliqué

Strips of assorted fabric scraps, or approximately ½ yard of fabric, in coordinating blacks for the scrap appliqué

⅛ yard of fabric for sign pole

2 yards of fusible web

12 extra-large eyelets (⅞6″) with tools (Dritz kit #660-65)

Base

All seams are ¼″ unless otherwise noted.

1. Measure from the top of your shower curtain rod to the floor, or the height you wish your finished curtain to be. Add 10″ to this measurement.

   Formula: finished curtain height + 10″ = cut height

2. Decide which side you want to be the bottom of your sheet. I used the large hem at the top of the sheet for the bottom of the shower curtain.

3. From the opposite end, trim off any fabric in excess of the cut height measurement you determined in Step 1.

   Example: If the sheet measures 92″ in length and the cut height is 90″, cut off 2″ from the length of the sheet.

4. Fold the cut edge under to the wrong side 5″ and press. Fold under again 5″ and press. Topstitch with a ¼″ seam allowance along both folded edges to finish the top of the curtain.

5. Depending on the size of the queen sheet, the spacing between the eyelets may differ. Measure the width of the shower curtain and space the eyelets evenly. To start, use a fabric pencil and mark a dot 2″ from the top of the curtain and 4″ from each side.

6. Continue to add the remaining 10 dots 2″ from the top and approximately 7″–8½″ apart. You should have 12 dots along the top of the curtain.

7. Following the manufacturer's instructions, install an eyelet at each of the 12 dots, centering the eyelet on the dot.

Scrap Appliqué

See Creating Scrap Appliqué (page 13) for detailed instructions. The Railroad Crossing patterns are on pages 99–101. They are reversed for fusible scrap appliqué.

1. Group the colored strips by color. Sew each color group of strips together to achieve approximately the following sizes:

    Black: 7½″ × width of fabric (Note that I placed the black letters sideways on the strips.)

    Cream: 2 strips each 5½″ × 33″

2. Press the seam allowances all the same direction on each color set.

    Optional: Topstitch the seams down.

3. Trim both cream strips to 4½″ × 32″.

4. Trace the Railroad Crossing patterns onto the paper side of the fusible web.

5. Loosely cut around each of the fusible web templates. Position the traced templates and iron them to the back of the black fabrics.

6. Carefully cut out the fused templates on the traced lines, and remove the paper backing. Fuse the appliqués in place on the cream fabric. Position the letters to spell RAIL ROAD on the first strip and CROSSING on the other. *Be sure to leave enough space to fit CROSSING between RAIL and ROAD. (Refer to the photo, page 96.)*

7. Fuse the fusible web to the entire back of the 2 cream strips. Remove the paper backing.

8. Measure and cut 2½″ × width of fabric from the fabric for the sign pole. Fuse the fusible web to the entire back of the strip. Trim the sign pole to 2″ wide. Remove the paper backing.

9. Lay the sheet out on a large flat surface or on the floor. Position the appliqué pieces on the sheet, slightly off center.

10. Start by lining up the pole with the hem or bottom of the curtain and extending it upward. Press into place.

11. Center the 2 cream appliqué strips in an X covering about ½˝ of the top of the pole. The 2 strips should be perpendicular to each other and at a 45° angle to the pole. Position the RAIL ROAD appliqué strip on the bottom and CROSSING on the top. Press into place.

12. Machine appliqué around the pieces with your favorite stitch. (I chose a small buttonhole stitch.)

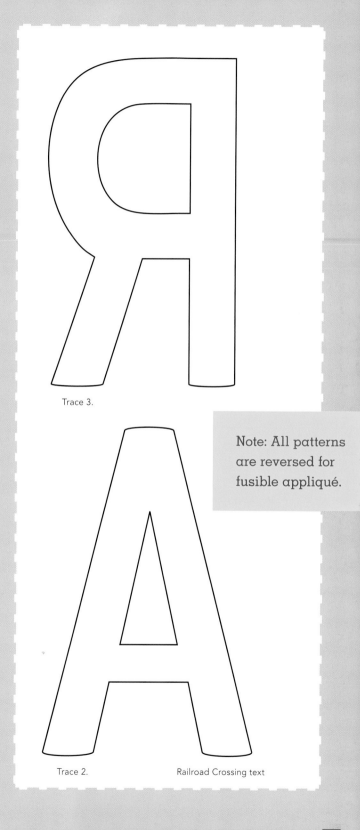

Trace 3.

Note: All patterns are reversed for fusible appliqué.

Trace 2.

Railroad Crossing text

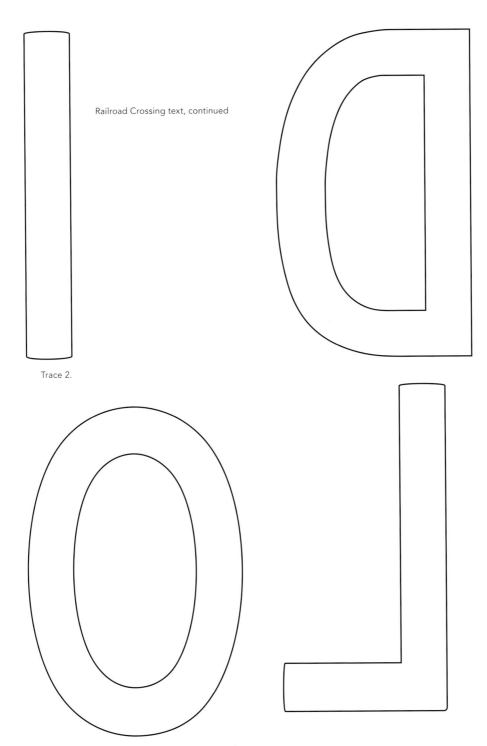

Railroad Crossing text, continued

Trace 2.

Trace 2.

Trace 2.

Super-simple raw-edge appliqués added to the bottom band of towels are a cute and fun way to add a little spark to the bathroom.

Cross Guard
TOWELS

Materials

Bath and hand towels

Strips of assorted fabric scraps in coordinating reds at least 16″ long for the scrap appliqués, in total about ½ yard

Assorted fabric scraps in coordinating creams at least 8″ long for the scrap appliqués, in total about ¼ yard

¾ yard of fusible web

Scrap Appliqué

See Creating Scrap Appliqué (page 13) for detailed instructions. The following directions are for decorating a bath towel with a 2½″ × 30″ band.

1. Group the colored strips by color. Sew each color group of strips together to achieve approximately the following sizes:

   Red: 16″ × 16″

   Cream: 8″ × 8″

2. Press the seam allowances in the same direction on each color set.

   Optional: Topstitch the seams down.

3. Fuse the fusible web to the wrong side of the scraps.

4. Most towels come with a presewn band along the bottom. Measure the band's height and width for each size of towel.

   Example: The band on the bath towel in this example measures 2½″ × 30″.

5. From the red base, cut 3 or 4 parallel strips at a 45° angle and spaced 2½˝ apart. Then subcut parallel to the direction of the sewn fabric strips to get 5 or 6 pieces that look like diamonds.

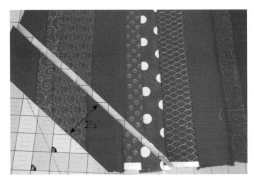

First cuts on diagonal

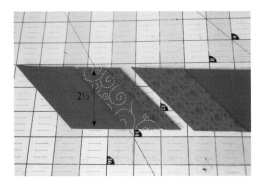

Subcut to make diamond shapes.

6. From the cream base, cut 3–4 strips that are perpendicular to the direction of the strips and 2½˝ wide. Then subcut on a 45° angle to make 5–6 diamond shapes.

7. Remove the paper backing from the diamond shapes, and line them up side by side, alternating the colors from red to cream to red. Each piece should overlap its neighboring piece by approximately ¼˝. Repeat this step until you have reached the opposite end of the band.

8. Trim the 2 end pieces to line up with the towel. Press all the pieces into place.

9. Using a straight stitch, machine appliqué the pieces down about ⅛˝ in on all sides of every piece. Wash to allow the edges to fray.

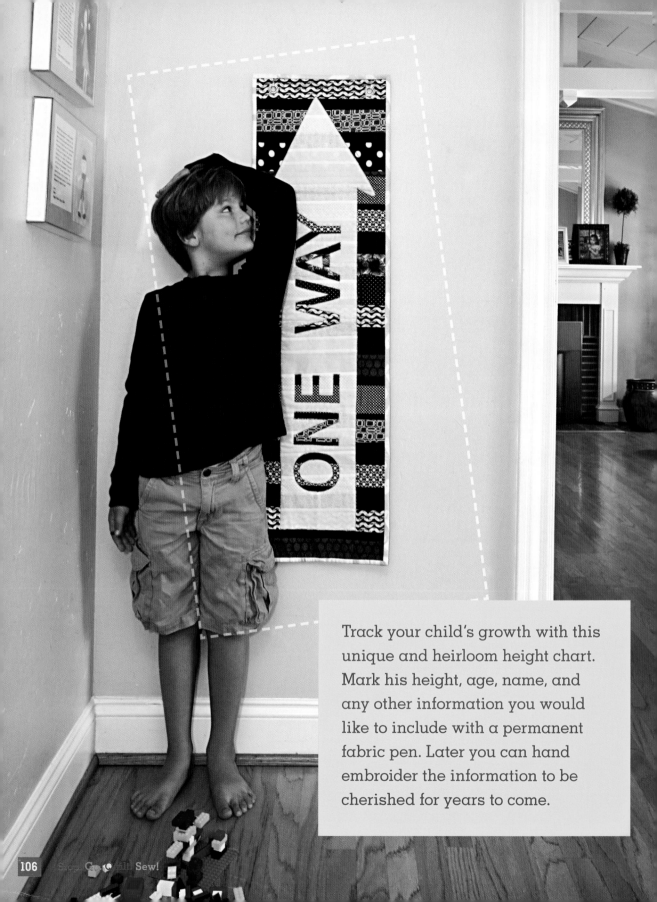

Track your child's growth with this unique and heirloom height chart. Mark his height, age, name, and any other information you would like to include with a permanent fabric pen. Later you can hand embroider the information to be cherished for years to come.

One Way
GROWTH CHART

Finished size: APPROXIMATELY 13″ × 43″

Materials

Strips of assorted fabric scraps at least 14″ long, or approximately 1 yard total, of blacks for the base fabric

Strips of assorted fabric scraps at least 12″ long, or approximately 1 yard total, of creams for the scrap appliqué

½ yard of coordinating fabric for backing (minimum 43″ wide)

⅜ yard of coordinating fabric for binding

2½ yards of fusible web

16″ × 45″ quilt batting

2 extra-large eyelets (⁷⁄₁₆″) with tools (Dritz kit #660-65)

Base

All seams are ¼″ unless otherwise noted.

1. Sew the black fabric scraps together to create a base fabric for the appliqués approximately 14″ × 44″.

2. Press all the seam allowances in the same direction.

3. Trim the piece from Step 2 to 13″ × 43″ for the base fabric for the scrap appliqués.

Scrap Appliqué

See Creating Scrap Appliqué (page 13) for detailed instructions. One Way patterns are on pullout page P4 and are reversed for fusible scrap appliqué. Use the reverse appliqué method (page 15) for this project.

1. Sew the cream strips together to achieve a size of about 13″ × 43″.

2. Press the seam allowances in the same direction on each color set.

   Optional: Topstitch the seams down.

3. Trim the unit from Step 2 to 12″ × 42″.

4. Trace the One Way patterns onto the paper side of the fusible web.

5. Loosely cut around each of the fusible web templates. Position and iron the traced templates to the backside of the cream fabrics.

6. Carefully cut out the fused templates on the traced lines. Cut on the arrow outline and on the letter outlines (part of the reverse appliqué method), and discard the letters or use them in another project. Remove the paper backing from the remaining cream fabric appliqué. Fuse the cream appliqué in place on the base fabric.

Finishing

1. Sandwich the backing fabric, batting, and quilt top together and safety pin all the layers together.

2. Machine appliqué around the pieces with your favorite stitch. I chose a small buttonhole stitch.

3. Using a rotary cutter, mat, and ruler, square up and trim off any excess fabric from all 4 sides of the quilt. Be sure all sides are trimmed evenly and the arrow is centered to your liking.

4. From the binding fabric, cut 4 strips 2½″ × width of fabric. Trim off all the selvages.

5. Refer to Binding (page 16) to create the binding and bind the quilt.

6. Following the manufacturer's instructions, attach 2 extra-large eyelets to the top corners of the growth chart for easy hanging. Eyelets should be placed 1½″ from the top and 2″ from each side.

About the Author

As a young girl, Angela Yosten was influenced by many talented people. While her mother taught her how to sew and encouraged all things arts and crafts–related, her father taught her how to be independent and figure things out on her own. Her grandmothers and great-grandmother also influenced her with their special talents of knitting, sewing, and art. She has always enjoyed drawing, painting, and designing, but it was not until she had her own children that she was inspired to find her way back into the sewing room and discover her own style.

When she is not working as a web developer, she can most likely be found in her sewing room. She finds it thrilling when she can design something new for one of her children or decor for her home. She is often intrigued by everyday items and loves to explore different ways to translate them to fabric. Many of her designs and tutorials can be found on her blog (blog.angelayosten.com).

Most of all, she enjoys spending time with her family and cherishing every little moment life has to offer. She feels very fortunate to have such a wonderful husband and amazing children who support her obsession to design and who encourage everything that she aspires to do.

stashBOOKS®

fabric arts for a handmade lifestyle

If you're craving beautiful authenticity in a time of mass-production...Stash Books is for you. Stash Books is a line of how-to books celebrating fabric arts for a handmade lifestyle. Backed by C&T Publishing's solid reputation for quality, Stash Books will inspire you with contemporary designs, clear and simple instructions, and engaging photography.

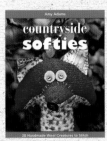

www.stashbooks.com